CW01183392

LIFE CYCLE OF A SHEEP

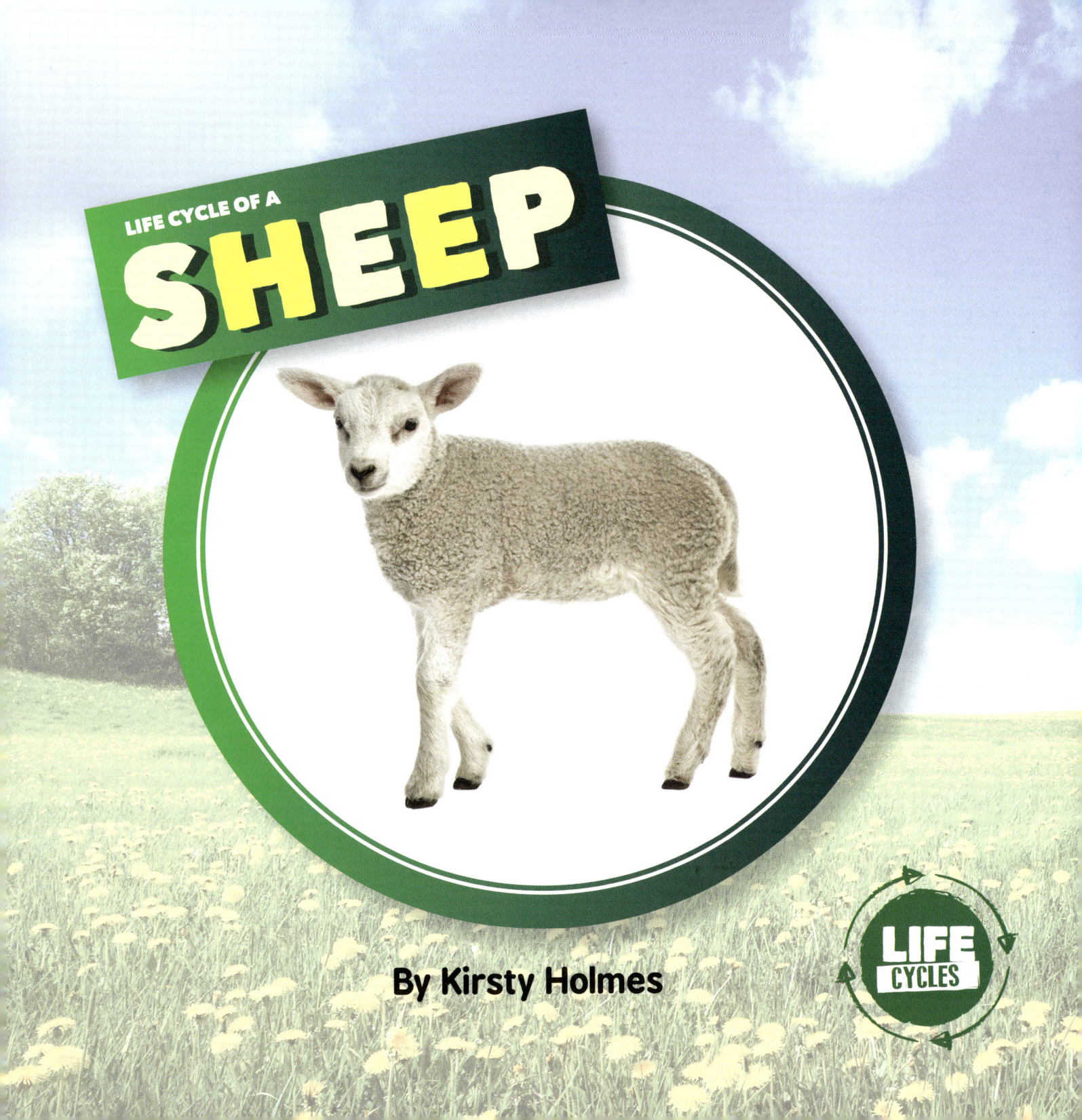

By Kirsty Holmes

LIFE CYCLES

Words that look like **this** can be found in the glossary on page 24.

BookLife PUBLISHING

©2021
BookLife Publishing Ltd.
King's Lynn
Norfolk PE30 4LS

ISBN: 978-1-83927-475-6

All rights reserved. Printed in Malta.

All facts, statistics, web addresses and URLs in this book were verified as valid and accurate at time of writing. No responsibility for any changes to external websites or references can be accepted by either the author or publisher.

Written by:
Kirsty Holmes

Edited by:
Shalini Vallepur

Designed by:
Brandon Mattless

A catalogue record for this book is available from the British Library.

PHOTO CREDITS

All images are courtesy of shutterstock.com, unless otherwise specified. With thanks to Getty Images, Thinkstock Photo and iStockphoto. Front Cover & 1 – Eric Isselee, LeManna. 2–3 – Simon Lees. 4–5 – hanapon1002, natu, paulaphoto, sunabesyou, ucchie79, violetblue. 6–7 – N-sky, photomaster. 8–9 – Emily Goodwin, julie deshaies. 10–11 – Coatesy, Holly Kuchera. 12–13 – Liz Miller, marilyn barbone. 14–15 – Nataliia Melnychuk, slowmotiongli. 16–17 – chris kolaczan, Dalibor Sevaljevic. 18–19 – Galina Savina, Pazargic Liviu, Tom Bird. 20–21 – Jodie Nash, Tomas Hulik ARTpoint. 22–23 – bogdanhoda, Emily Goodwin, FOTOGRIN, Melinda Nagy, William John Hunter.

LIFE CYCLE OF A SHEEP

Page 4	**What Is a Life Cycle?**
Page 6	**Super Sheep**
Page 8	**Perfect Pregnancy**
Page 10	**Little Lambs**
Page 12	**Lively Lambs**
Page 14	**Soft Sheep!**
Page 16	**Life as a Sheep**
Page 18	**Fun Facts about Sheep**
Page 20	**The End of Life as a Sheep**
Page 22	**The Life Cycle**
Page 24	**Glossary and Index**

WHAT IS A LIFE CYCLE?

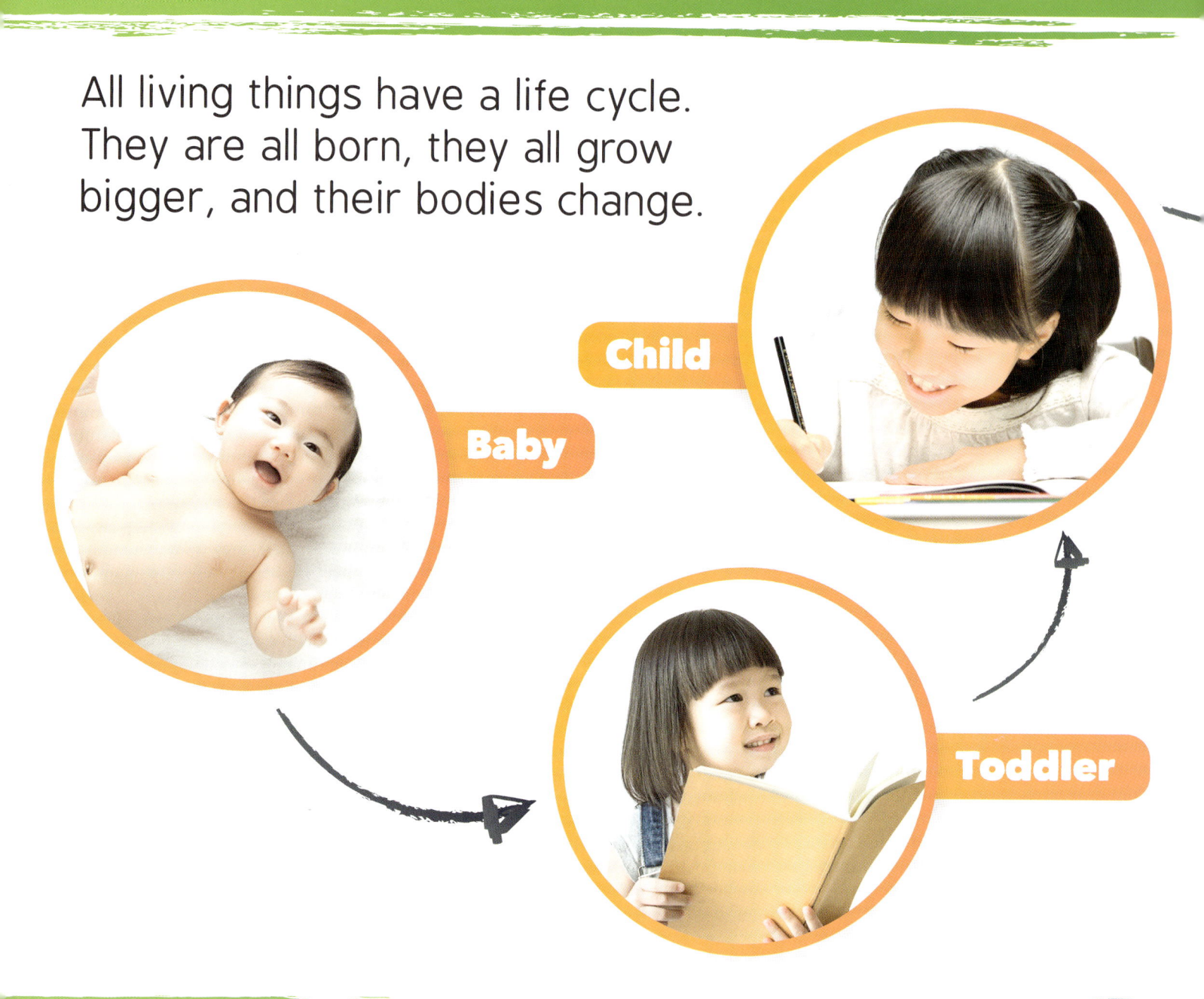

All living things have a life cycle. They are all born, they all grow bigger, and their bodies change.

Baby

Child

Toddler

When they are fully grown, they have **offspring** of their own. In the end, all living things die. This is the life cycle.

Teenager

Adult

Elderly person

SUPER SHEEP

Sheep are **mammals**. They have four legs and are covered in thick wool. Sheep have short tails.

Tail

Horns

Wool

Legs

Male sheep are called rams. Rams usually have horns on their heads.

Female sheep are called ewes. Some ewes have horns and some do not.

Sheep are herbivores. This means they only eat plants. Some sheep are **wild**, but most sheep live on farms. These sheep have been **domesticated**.

PERFECT PREGNANCY

A female sheep will **mate** with a male sheep. She will become pregnant. This means baby sheep will grow inside her belly.

Pregnant Belly

A ewe will have between one and three babies. Most ewes have two babies, called twins.

When the mother has her babies, it is called lambing.

Ewes are pregnant for about five months. During this time, the mother sheep's belly will get bigger, showing she is carrying her growing babies.

LITTLE LAMBS

Lambs can walk and drink milk from their mother when they are born.

Lambs are usually born in the spring. When a lamb is born, it learns the sound and smell of its mother. This way, it can always find her in the **flock**.

Young lambs are fluffy and playful. They love to run and skip. Usually, a baby sheep is called a lamb until it is one year old.

LIVELY LAMBS

Lambs grow very quickly and love to explore. They will sniff and nibble new things to find out about them.

Lambs like to climb on their mothers and play. Sheep live in groups, called flocks, and like to stay together.

SOFT SHEEP!

Adult sheep will reach their full size and will grow thick, woolly fleeces. Some sheep wool is even curly!

Fleece

Adult sheep are ready to have babies of their own. They will mate and the ewe will become pregnant. The life cycle continues.

Ram

Ewe

Lamb

15

LIFE AS A SHEEP

The bighorn is a type of sheep that lives in the Rocky Mountains.

Wild sheep usually live on hills or mountains. They do not look like domestic sheep. Their fleeces have a mixture of wool and hair.

Sheep that live on farms give us wool, milk and meat. The farmer **shears** the fleece off in the warmer months and it is turned into **yarn**.

Yarn can be used to make clothing such as jumpers and socks.

FUN FACTS ABOUT SHEEP

- Sheep can remember the faces of many other sheep – plus their shepherd's voice.

Shepherd

- Sheep can show their feelings on their faces – and understand other sheep's feelings too!

- The largest type of wild sheep is the Argali sheep. Adult rams can be 125 centimetres tall and can weigh over 140 kilograms!

THE END OF LIFE AS A SHEEP

Domesticated sheep can live for around ten years. As a sheep gets older, it won't grow as much wool and it may lose its teeth.

Wild sheep use their horns to protect themselves against **predators**. Wild sheep have good eyesight and a strong sense of smell to help them avoid a fight.

Wolves, bears, eagles and wild cats all like to hunt sheep.

THE LIFE CYCLE

Pregnancy

Newborn

A sheep's life cycle has different stages. Each stage looks very different from the last.

Lamb

Sheep

The ewe is pregnant for five months. She will have one to three lambs that will grow quickly. Adult sheep are ready to mate and have babies of their own.

In the end, the sheep dies, and the life cycle is complete.

23

GLOSSARY

domesticated   when an animal has been tamed and can be kept by humans

flock   a group of the same type of animals that stay together

mammals   animals that are warm-blooded, have a backbone and make milk to feed their children

mate   make young animals with another animal of the same type

offspring   the babies of an animal or plant

predators   animals that hunt other animals for food

shears   cuts the hair or wool off of an animal

wild   living in nature without human control or care

yarn   thread that is made from wool

INDEX

domestic 7, 16, 20
ewes 7–9, 15, 23
flocks 10, 13

horns 6–7, 21
lambs 9–12, 15, 23
milk 10, 17

rams 6, 15, 19
wild 7, 16, 19, 21
wool 6, 14, 16–17, 20